Señor Felipe's Alphabet Adventure

El Alfabeto Español

Written & Illustrated
by Sharon Hawkins Vargo

Spanish Translations by Ann Kelly Beale

THE MILLBROOK PRESS INC.

Brookfield, Connecticut

For Mom and Dad with love, SHV

Library of Congress Cataloging-in-Publication Data
Vargo, Sharon Hawkins.
Señor Felipes alphabet adventure: el alfabeto Español/by Sharon Hawkins Vargo.
p. cm.
Summary: Señor Felipe is given the mission to photograph things
that begin with each letter of the Spanish alphabet.
ISBN 0-7613-1860-7 (lib. bdg.) ISBN 0-7613-1897-6 (pbk.)
[1. Alligators—Fiction. 2. Spanish language—
Alphabet—Fiction. 3. Alphabet.] I. Title.
PZ7.V442Se2001 [E]—dc21
99-048491

Published by The Millbrook Press, Inc.
2 Old New Milford Road
Brookfield, Connecticut 06804
www.millbrookpress.com

Text and illustrations copyright © 2001
by Sharon Hawkins Vargo
Printed in the United States of America
All rights reserved
LIB. BDG. 5 4 3 2 1
PAPERBACK 5 4 3 2 1

Flip back to this map to check your place during the adventure.

In a cozy hut on
a remote island
lives a photographer named Señor Felipe.
Paco, his trusty parrot, checks the mailbox
each day hoping for an assignment.

Paco wakes Señor Felipe from a siesta to give him a letter. It's an assignment!

In a cozy hut on
a remote island
lives a photographer named Señor Felipe.
Paco, his trusty parrot, checks the mailbox
each day hoping for an assignment.

Paco wakes Señor Felipe from a siesta to give
him a letter. It's an assignment!

Señor Felipe and Paco begin their picture-taking adventure.

Señor Felipe
Fotógrafo

Walk past the **tree**.

A

el árbol (ARH bol)

Step into the **small boat**. **B** la barca (BAR ka)

Bump! Boom! The **truck** is ready.

C el camión (cah me OHN)

Dont forget the **jacket**.

CH

la chaqueta (cha KE ta)

Pay the **money** for parking.

D el dinero (dee NE ro)

Climb the **staircase**.

E

la escalera
(es ca LEH ra)

Smell the **flowers**.

F

las flores (FLO res)

Señor?

Pay the **money** for parking.

D el dinero (dee NE ro)

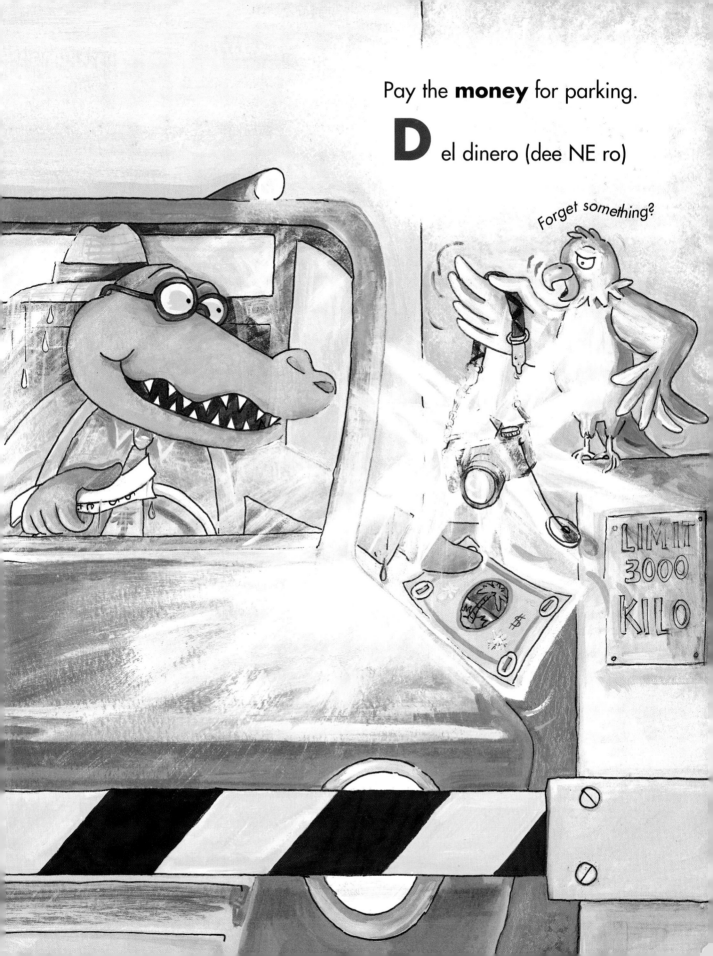

Climb the **staircase**.

E

la escalera
(es ca LEH ra)

Smell the **flowers**.

F

las flores (FLO res)

Señor?

Spy the **cat**.

G

el gato (GAH toe)

Enjoy the
ice cream.

H

el helado (eh LA doe)

Tiptoe past the **church**.

la iglesia (ee GLAY sya)

Rest in the **garden**.

J

el jardín (har DEEN)

Stop at the **newsstand**. K el kiosco (KYOS ko)

Buy the **book**. L el libro (LEE bro)

Watch out for the **garden hose**!

M

la manguera (man GE ra)

See the **cloud**...

N

la nube (NU bay)

This is getting dangerous!

and the **gnu**.

Ñ

el ñu (nyu)

Shut the **door**.

P

la puerta (PWER ta)

Whoops! There goes
the **cheese**.

Q

el queso (KAY so)

CAUTION
WET
FLOOR

Look out for the **bull**!

T

el toro (TOH ro)

Run for your life!

Don't trample the **grapes**!

U

las uvas (OO bas)

What a funny show for the **cow**!

V la vaca
(BAH ka)

The **xylophone** tips.
Bing! Bong!

X

el xilófono
(si LO fo no)

Wear the **helmet**.

Y

el yelmo (YEL mo)

Zoom past
the **shoes**!

Z

los zapatos
(sa PA toes)

Assignment complete!
Can you remember the Spanish word
for each photograph?

Your assignment is to find the Spanish vocabulary throughout Señor Felipe's Adventure. Good Luck! → Paco

A

el agua (A gwa)
water

los anteojos
(an tay OH hos)
eyeglasses

B

el bocadillo
(bo ka DEE yo)
sandwich

el botón
(bo TONE)
button

C

la cámara fotográfica
(KA ma ra
fo toe GRA fee ka)
camera

la carta (KAR ta)
letter

la corbata
(kor BAH ta)
necktie

CH

el champú (cham PU)
shampoo

el charco
(CHAR ko)
puddle

la choza (CHO sah)
hut

D

los dientes
(dee EN tays)
teeth

el dulce
(DUL say)
candy

E

el este (ES tay)
east

la estrella
(es TRAY ya)
star

F

la foca (FO ka)
seal

la fotografía
(fo toe gra FEE a)
photograph

G

la gallina
(gah YEE na)
hen

el globo
(GLO bo)
balloon

H

la hormiga
(or MEE gah) ant

la huella (WAY ya)
footprint

el humo (OO mo)
smoke

I

la iguana
(ee GWA na)
iguana

la isla (EES lah)
island

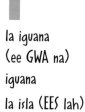

J

el jabón
(ha BONE) soap

K

el kilo (KEE lo) kilo

L

el lápiz
(LAH pees)
pencil

la luna
(LU na)
moon

LL

la llanta
(YAN ta)
tire

la lluvia
(YU bee a)
rain

M

la mano (MA no)
hand

la mesa (MAY sah)
table

la montaña
(mon TAHN ya)
mountain

N

la noche (NO chay)
night

el norte (NOR tay)
north

Ñ

el ñandú
(nyan DU)

ostrich

O

el oeste
(o ES tay) west

los ojos
(O hos)

eyes

la ola
(O lah)

wave

P

el pájaro (PA ha ro)
bird

el pie (PEE ay)
foot

la pluma
(PLU ma)

feather

Q

el quitasol
(ki ta SOL)

parasol

R

la rana (RRA na)
frog

el ratón (rra TONE)

mouse

S

el sello
(SAY yo) postage

stamp

la serpiente
(ser pee EN tay)

snake

el sol
(SOL)

sun

el sombrero
(som BRE ro)

hat

el sur (SUR)
south

T

el tenedor
(te ne DOR)

table fork

el tiesto
(tee ES toe)

flower pot

U

la umbría
(oom BREE a) shadow

V

el vaso (BAH so)
drinking glass

la ventana
(ben TAH na) window

X

X–26th letter of
the Spanish alphabet

Y

el yerbajo
(yer BAH ho) weed

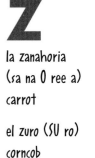

Z

la zanahoria
(sa na O ree a)

carrot

el zuro (SU ro)
corncob

About the Author/Artist

Look for more exciting adventures from author/artist Sharon Vargo. A graduate of Pratt Institute, she lives in a remote part of Indianapolis with her husband, four teenage sons, and a trusty parakeet. Ms. Vargo is the illustrator of many beginning readers and the Millbrook Press title, *Make Yourself a Monster* by Kathy Ross.